Dragonfly Magic

Poems by
Dwayne Cole

Dragonfly Magic
ISBN: Softcover 978-1-951472-98-6
Copyright © 2021 by Dwayne Cole

All rights reserved. No part of this book may be reproduced or transmitted in any form or by any means, electronic or mechanical, including photocopying, recording, or by any information storage and retrieval system, without permission in writing from the publisher.

Parson's Porch Books is an imprint of Parson's Porch & Company (PP&C) in Cleveland, Tennessee. PP&C is an innovative organization which raises money by publishing books of noted authors, representing all genres. Its face and voice is **David Russell Tullock** (dtullock@parsonsporch.com).

Parson's Porch & Company *turns books into bread & milk* by sharing its profits with the poor.

www.parsonsporch.com

Dragonfly Magic

Contents

Dedication	7
Preface	9
Introduction to Dragonfly Magic	10
Poetry is a Love Knot	14
Dragonfly Shadow	19
Red Saddleback Dragonfly Limerick	21
Green Darners	23
Dear Mister Dragonfly	25
Dragonfly Haiku	28
Dragonfly Efficiency	30
Nature's Rare Gift	33
Red Light Blinking	39
Yellow Caution Light	41
Dragonflies Burst into Flight	44
Caution Light	46
Rainbow Wings	48
Dragonfly Song	50
Hope	51
Four Wings	53
Metamorphosis	55
Dragonfly Wings of Hope and Love	57
Conclusion	60
Dragonfly Haibun	61
Concluding Good Luck Dragonfly Poem	62
Other Books By Dwayne Cole	64

Dedication

This book is dedicated to my good friend, George Wilbur Reid. For the past decade he has sent me inspiring photos taken on his daily walks through beautiful Florida. These dragonfly photos magically flew to Alaska on angel wings, bringing Florida sunshine to Alaska, often on dark snowy days with total darkness. Darkness blooms and sings. Life is more luminous and filled with meaning when dragonfly gems are glimmering. I returned the favor by sending him ekphrastic wonder poems inspired by his art. All the photos are Wilbur's creative work.

Preface

As kingfishers catch fire, dragonflies draw flame.
—Gerard Manly Hopkins

For many centuries
in many parts of the world

the dragonfly has been a symbol of hope
and new beginnings

In Native American legends
the dragonfly is a symbol

of transformation
and renewal after hardship

Its magical iridescence
invites the discovery of one's own colors

Unmasking the real self
giving a confident sense of identity

Light on me,
Mr. Dragonfly bring me good luck.

Introduction to Dragonfly Magic

"And above all, watch with glittering eyes the whole world around you because the greatest secrets are always hidden in the most unlikely places. Those who don't believe in magic will never find it.
-Roald Dahl

I loved being outside as a child
playing at the mill rock's
flowing sparkling stream

dragonflies flitting about catching fire
catch the beauty in a net
Release and pretend it was a rainbow.

Dragonflies can be placed
in the same category
as butterflies and other angel winged gifts of nature.

However to place them in a group
called angel wings
is a bit of poetic license

Their Greek name, anisoptera, means unequal wings—
The back two wings are broader
than the front two.

The Latin name, teneral, does imply tender,
but this is more to indicate the fragile nature of their life cycle,
than to signify their gentle behavior.

In fact, the dragonfly begins life as a nymph
and lives by eating other nymphs
for six months to four years, depending on species,

and if it luckily avoids
getting eaten by a rainbow trout
for some other predator.

During its water life,
the nymph molts its skin
up to a dozen times.

Completing its growth process,
it swims to the surface and anchors itself to a root or stem
where it undergoes metamorphosis.

It sits and waits for its wings to dry.
After a few hours, the adult dragonfly
is an aerial acrobat.

If dragonflies are able to avoid predators,
they can live up to six months.
However, many live only a few weeks after gaining wings.

Dragonflies are wonders of nature,
emerging from flowing time with
eternity in those large eyes

An aerial acrobat,
Memory flashes of light.
Zipping forward, sideways, backward.

Oh the fragile nature of their life cycle—
There's a saying,
"We often don't know what we've got until it's gone!"

Do we need to destroy dragonfly's haven
for one more strip mall,
one more parking lot?

If we destroy the planet
who will remember
these winged beauties?

Before it is too late, this book seeks
to kindle wonder
for these dancing on the wind acrobatic gems.

Poetry is a Love Knot

Two dragonflies tangled
in a love knot

Hold on as they bang
art page wings

Eight wings fanning
flame of desire

Dancers floating
Eternity's golden moments

Settle on a flower stem
Rapidly sipping

Quivering as one
Not wanting to part

Who would have thought
Love could be so easy

Causing me to ponder
Muse in deep thought

How many kinds of love are there
in our diverse universe

Tenderness freely given
Tenderness willingly received

Wisdom is receiving gift given
Celebrate tenderness!

Dragonfly Shadow

Does the dragonfly know
It is a dragonfly?

I wonder.

Which is real?
The tangible angel wings
that flap like pages in an art book

or, the intangible shadow
cast on the green
lily landing pad?

I wonder.

Getting their next meal,
the dragonfly preys on
smaller, weaker insects.

An action more akin
to the dark shadow
than to angel wings.

An action reminiscent of the dragon
of the Apocalypse of John
pursuing the woman and eating her child.

Does the dragonfly know
that he has a dark shadow side,

A jinn like goblin with a spin,
propelling him from within?

A tirade, a fusillade, a gulp!
One friendly enemy down.

Causing me to ponder
Carl Jung's famous dictum:

Is the shadow in humans
the source of all coming evil?

I wonder.

Red Saddleback Dragonfly Limerick

Once there was a red dragonfly
A saddlebag flapping in sky
Art book pages turning
Bright blue eyes yearning
Angel wings do not deify

Green Darners

Dragonfly flights are cancelled
due to heavy rain.
Please come again.

Don't wait too late.
My season passes fast.
I have left only one date.

(Green Darners—
Using ratio of hydrogen isotopes found in wings,
researchers can determine the approximate birth ponds
of some of the most abundant laggards.

Laggard means that geneticists now believe that dragonflies
have not changed in the last two hundred million years.
A dragonfly can travel 1000 miles on its two inch wings,
from Canada to the Gulf of Mexico.
They rarely migrate in large swarms.
Up close the Green Darners are radiant,
with emerald green thorax
and splashes of blue on abdomen.)

Dear Mister Dragonfly

Ring a Ding Ding
You've got shiny golden wings

Sliced and diced
perfectly spiced

Come show me how to swing
Show me how to sing

Oh sweet, Mister Dragonfly
Can't we fly away

Birds in bloom
seeds in flight

All sun, all fun, all frolic
All night

No more dreary,
no more gray

Radiant beams
stream all day

Party, party
skip, skip, hop

Party, party
Champagne pop

Bubble, bubble zip
I want an aerobatic flip

In my pocket, in my wocket
In my inner glowing socket

Light me up,
pop my ping

Light me up,
make me zing

One tiny way
One big flight

One shiny day
One zoom-bah night

Can't we
Dear Mister Dragonfly

Oh sweet, Mister Dragonfly
Just one tiny day

Dragonfly Haiku

First time perfection
Millions of years unchanged
Genes know a keeper

Dragonfly Efficiency

When God designed the dragonflies,
I was not consulted.
were you?

Efficiency put to test—

Geneticists believe
dragonflies have not changed
in the last two hundred million years.

When a dragonfly
sets its sight on prey,
95% of the time dinner is served.

Better than my casting a fly
for a rainbow trout.

I often cast 100 times
to catch one rainbow!

Nature's Rare Gift

Two hundred million years
genetically coded miracles
rainbows of color.

This laggard species
dries in the sun a few hours
and lifts into flight.

Waving its wings
Art pages flapping in sun
Beauty to behold.

Wonder unfolds!

Dragonfly beauty
Wafting to and fro in sky
Art book pages turn

Red Light Blinking

Warning all insects:
If you see this red light blink
better hit brakes.

If you do not stop
you will have dragon to pay.
His teeth are wicked.

His claws are sticky.
No insect is too yicky,
and he is tricky.

Cannibalistic---
he eats his own kin
with grin.

He will bite you too.
But only when trapped
Wanting to be free

Zigging and zagging
In the gentle breeze
To avoid change

Yellow Caution Light

Some have red headlights
some have green
If you see either of these
treat both as yellow

Go with great caution
Or your wreck will be fatal
I never said nature is always kind!

Dragonflies Burst into Flight

Genetically coded rainbows of color
emerge from dark gray water nymph.

Dry in the sun a few hours
and burst into flight!

Caution Light

Yellow light flashing
Means caution to smaller things.
I eat my own kin.

Rainbow Wings

The dragon fly,
a marvel of nature,
with shimmering rainbow wings and
lightning bolt running through the elongated body,
a thing of beauty.

Known as a teneral,
Latin for "tender, soft or delicate."
After a few hours of molting and drying in the sun
the adult dragonfly is an aerial acrobat,
a dazzling light show.

An elfin with jinn spin
in the dancing sun.

If the weather is warm
and the dragonfly is able to avoid predators,
it can live up to six months.
However, many live only a few weeks.

Nature's gifts are so beautiful.
Maybe a few months of
flapping rainbow wings
like pages in an art book,

Just maybe that is enough.

Splendors in Grassy Waters

Beauties that stir wonder
Are ministers of delight

Bringing gifts of love
Setting the soul on fire.

Dragonfly Song

When the warm sunrise rays
fall on the gray dragonfly nymph
It crawls from the water onto a stem
and molts one final time

Its large eyes, forming 80%
of its head mass,
sees the sunlight gleaming
and stars streaming

Maneuvering with four wings
Each with its own muscles
Darting through the air
They call us to follow

Glimmering incandescence
Ribbons of rainbow colors
glimmer glimmer
Inspiring in us new hope and love.

Shine dragonfly wonder aglow
Shine dragonfly shimmer shimmer
Bring light for our darkness

Lead us on luminous wings of love
Such a magic feeling
to zig zag with rainbow wings

Above us
Within us
Shine with glowing love.

Hope

The dragonfly's eyes take up almost 80%
of the volume of their head

With nearly 360 degree field of view
enabling them to keep track of objects in their sight

Dragonflies have four separately controllable wings
the second pair of wings are used as gyroscopes to control their flight

They move with elegance and grace
with computer skills developed for millions of years

Part II

For many centuries
in many parts of the world

the dragonfly has been a symbol of hope
and new beginnings

In Native American legends
the dragonfly is a symbol

of transformation
and renewal after hardship

Its magical iridescence
invites the discovery of one's own colors

Unmasking the real self
giving a confident sense of identity

Light on me, Mr Dragonfly
bringing me good luck.

Four Wings

If I had four wings as dragonflies
I would fly like Noah's dove
to the olive branch of peace and love

Bringing peace on earth
Kindness to all.

Metamorphosis

In the rapid metamorphosis
from nymph to adult dragonfly

We are inspired to change
Move with the flow

Plunge right in
Join the rainbow dance

Shimmering with
incandescence

Resurrection
to adventurous new life

Dragonfly Wings of Hope and Love

When the sunrise warm rays
fall on the gray dragonfly nymph
it crawls from the water onto a stem
and molts one final time

Its large eyes
red blue green
see sunlight gleaming
stars streaming

Maneuvering with four wings
each with its own muscles
darting through the air
they call us to follow

Glimmering incandescence
ribbons of rainbow colors
glimmer glimmer
inspiring in us new hope and love

Shine dragonfly wonder aglow
shine dragonfly shimmer shimmer
bring light for our darkness
lead us on wings of love.

Conclusion

Oh please, put down your iPhone and go sit on a lily pad with a dragonfly. Maybe a red saddleback. Take a spin. Be a Jennie for a while. A little magic can carry you a long way in life. A little frolicking now and then is enjoyed by the wisest.

I hope you will also share this book with your children and grandchildren. You never know how a love of nature will change and transform lives for the good.

Dragonfly Haibun

As a young boy,
George Church spent time wading in the mudflats of Tampa Bay
hunting for insects. Exploring one day, he found a little submarine with legs.
George put it in a jar, and he was in awe the next day
when he saw it had metamorphosed into a dragonfly.
This thrilling experience set him on the path to being a biologist
at Harvard and playing a key role in code breaking genetic discoveries.

Metamorphosis
Egg nymph molting many times
Dragonfly emerges

Concluding Good Luck Dragonfly Poem

For many centuries
in many parts of the world

the Dragonfly has been a symbol of hope
and new beginnings

In Native American
legends the dragonfly is a symbol

of transformation
and renewal after hardship

Its magical iridescence
invites the discovery of one's own colors

Unmasking the real self
giving a confident sense of identity

Light on ALL OF US, Mr Dragonfly
bringing US ALL good luck!

Other Books By Dwayne Cole

A Center that Holds: Adventures in Kindness.
A Prayer of Blessing: As You Go Remember This.
A Relational Hermeneutic of Kindness.
A Relational Trinity of Kindness.
Bears and Moose of Alaska: Nature Poetry
Down on the Farm in Georgia: A Poetic Memoir
Gentle Galilean Glories: The Tender Teachings of Jesus
God and Evil: An Ode to Kindness.
Jesus' Transforming Beatitudes: Selected Sermons from Year A.
Jesus' Transforming Love: Selected Sermons from Year B.
Jesus' Transforming Gentle Teachings: Selected Sermons from Year C.
Kindness Is Every Step
Poems Inspired by Process Philosophy
Poet of the Universe: A Vision of Beauty and Goodness
The Apostles' Creed: A Living Creed for the Living Church.
The Book of Revelation: Jesus' Kindness Transforms Suffering.
The Serenity Prayer: A Pathway to Peace and Happiness.
The Story of the Bible: Authority, Inspiration, Canonization, and Translation.
TREES AND DRIFTWOOD: Poetic Ecology
WINGS OF INSPIRATION

www.ingramcontent.com/pod-product-compliance
Lightning Source LLC
Chambersburg PA
CBHW042101120526
44592CB00026B/14